I AM HER

ALISHA COLLINS

TABLE OF CONTENTS

DEDICATION

I dedicate this book to the like-minded woman currently reading this book. God sees you and He knows you want to make some big changes in your life. Reading this book will allow you to start making those changes, so you can become the best woman God wants you to be!

———————

INTRODUCTION

Sis, I am so glad you chose to read this book! Reading this book will be life-changing for you, just as much as it was life-changing for me to write it. In this book, I will talk about different obstacles I have overcome and the tools I used to overcome them. These tools have allowed me to become closer to God, which made me into the transformed woman I am today. I want you to know that I am just like you, and it all started with a simple prayer that got me to where I am today. You too can become closer to God by just trusting and believing.

I want to tell my story and what I encountered between 2019 and 2020. In my story, I will talk about different situations and people that made me want a better relationship with God today. I am not here to bash anyone's character but to simply tell my story. My story will explain my journey and how I have overcome it with the help of God and how I made one of the best decisions of putting myself first, which has allowed me to be who I am today.

My goal is to help you with the process of becoming closer to God as well by explaining what worked for me. One tool that helped me throughout my journey that I will explain more in this book is journaling. Journaling has changed my life. So, throughout this book, you will have the privilege of reading a few of my authentic journal entries that explain my transformation between 2019 and 2020. I honestly never thought I would be a writer/author until God gave me the idea to start journaling. From my very first journal on September 3, 2019, I will explain any hurt, pain, and happy moments I have encountered. So, with the hopes of me explaining my journaling journey, you too can transform your life.

I consider myself The Real Manifesting Queen, so you will notice how I am manifesting my life, my future husband, and children, but that is for another book. I want to be open and transparent with my journaling journey because this is who I am. So, as I take you on my personal journaling journey, I pray I can touch you in a way that can be beneficial in your life.

On September 3, 2019, God gave me the word to start my journaling journey. During this time in 2019, I was at a place where I was transitioning from a toxic 5-year relationship to entering my single season. Not only was I leaving a 5-year relationship, but I was walking away from a friendship that I thought was genuine. With walking away from a relationship and friendship, you can only imagine how I felt, ALONE. I felt like I had no one because these two people were the ones I would go to when I had any problems. So, losing them was like losing my support system.

Very first Journal Entry:

September 3, 2019

NEEDING TO KNOW GOD'S WILL

"Trust in the Lord with all your heart, not on your own understanding. He will guide you on the right paths." - Proverbs 3:5-6 (HCSB)

Wow is all I can say! Just last Sunday (9/1/2019), I was feeling very emotional due to my recent breakup with Donnie. I went to church and planned to leave early but ended up staying the entire service. As others went up to get prayed for by the Pastor, I became very emotional and began to cry. I feel like the First Lady and Pastor noticed me being very emotional and he told me to take the long way around the church to come up to the altar to get prayed for. When I reached the front, I began to cry more. All he did was lay his hand on my forehead, and I continued to cry and shout. After that, I instantly felt *relieved. The pastor said to me, "Alisha, you are headed down the right path. It may not feel like it, but you are." That statement alone made me feel so proud. So, in stride with today's verse, He will guide you on the right paths and I believe that with all your heart. I just pray, Lord, lead me to the great things you want me to have! I will trust you with all my heart and not my own understanding because I do not understand at this moment. Amen.*

CHAPTER 1
DONNIE & I

Donnie and I were together for five years in total. At the beginning of our relationship, everything was great! We got along well and I thought marriage would be in our future. Things moved rather fast with us and we were inseparable while living together for only after a month. Not only were we living together, but we were working together, which turned out to be a recipe for disaster. With us living and working together, I developed this co-dependency relationship with Donnie, and I began to idolize him.

So, let me rewind back a little. When Donnie and I worked together, I noticed little things about him that I would consider red flags. I decided to ignore those red flags because I never had a man give me all this attention. I would notice that he still had some dealings with his ex-girlfriend, who happened to be the mother of his children. He would constantly tell me that they were no longer together and would stress to me that he was a single man. In the back of my mind, I felt that he was lying to me, but I hoped that maybe there was some truth to it.

So, with me continuing to ignore the red flags that I was noticing, we eventually began dating. At this time in my life, I barely had a relationship with God, so I did not have any guidance. I thought I had it all together because I had one of the most popular men at work and I was his main focus. I enjoyed the thought of other women being so envious of me because I had Donnie and they could not have him. I believed that I had almost everything and that Donnie was the missing piece I needed.

As time went on, Donnie and I spent more and more time together. Even though we worked two different shifts at work, we still managed to spend quality time together. He worked the day shift while I worked the evening shift, and he would often stay at work during the evening shift to work overtime to be with me. After the evening shift was over, we would go to his place to stay for the night. At this time, my life consisted of Donnie and work. That totally completed me.

We began to do everything together, and when I say "everything," I mean everything. You would not see me without him and vice versa. We worked, shopped, and did everything together. At this time, I was 26 and I felt like we could spend the rest of our lives together. I felt like I had everything figured out if I had Donnie by my side.

After years of Donnie and I being together, I began to see him for the man he truly was. I continued to idolize him and I put him before everyone else despite how he treated me. He began cheating and lying. Through it all, I still prioritized him. All the effort that I was putting into making him see me as wife material, I should have been putting into a relationship with God. I thought Donnie and I would be together forever, and I did not think I needed to engage in any relationship with God. I pushed God so far in the background of my life and never began a relationship with Him.

After being together for years with all the lies, cheating, and manipulation, I began to realize that this was not love. I realized that this man did not want to marry me and would never commit to me. I felt stuck and like I was wasting my time. I desired marriage and children and I felt as if he did not want that with me. I knew that God was pushing me to realize my true value at this point in my life. It wasn't long until I decided to develop a better relationship with Him. With my desire for marriage and a family of my own, I began to want a relationship with God as well. I was going to church more because I felt Donnie and I were headed in two different directions.

In the spring of 2018, I decided to give my life to the Lord and I could not have made a better choice for my life. God had different plans for my life, even though I thought I had it all figured out when Donnie and I were dating. I began to devote more of my time to God instead of consuming so much of my time thinking about if Donnie wanted to continue this relationship or not. After getting saved, I was determined to make things work with us even though Donnie felt different. While I was determined to make things work, Donnie was determined to be selfish and do his own thing.

In the midst of me trying to repair my relationship with God, Donnie had other plans of his own. Around this time, Donnie had just begun a new job, so we did not spend much time together anymore. He was working the evening shift while I was working the day shift at my job, and we saw less and less of each other. By the time he clocked out of work, I was in bed. I soon realized that he was spending a lot of time in his car after work, mainly talking on the phone, but I was usually too exhausted from work to keep up with

Donnie's whereabouts anymore. Donnie knew this about me and felt free to do what he pleased.

One time he mentioned that he was going out of town to Dallas, Texas, with a couple of his coworkers. I did not know these coworkers, but I decided to believe he was taking an innocent guy's trip to Texas. Before taking his trip, he asked to borrow $200 to take out of town to feel more comfortable with his expenses. I agreed and wanted to make sure he was ok in that department, so I lent him the money. He left for the trip, which was a Memorial Day weekend. I instantly began to feel that something was off.

Once he told me he arrived safely in Texas, I, unfortunately, did not hear from him for the remainder of the holiday weekend. This entire weekend, I remember feeling so empty and alone. I could not wrap my mind around why Donnie was behaving this way towards me. I began to blame myself. I asked myself things like, "Is it me? Is it because I gained a little weight? Or is it because we have not been as intimate as we used to due to him working the new job?" I could not figure it out, but I began to feel less of a woman.

Once he arrived back from this "All Guys Trip," he behaved as if nothing had happened. I remember him coming home, acting as if he really came from a trip with coworkers and like he did nothing wrong. Things were not sitting well with me, so I began to investigate. He was on my phone plan at the time, so I started to check his call history. As I searched, I noticed an out-of-town number that showed up numerous times on his call history. I was at work while checking the call history, so once it was time for my break, I made sure to reach out to this mysterious number.

While heading to break, I became so nervous because my gut was telling me that it was another female and she may have something to do with this "All Guys Trip." I got in my car and dialed the number. Low and behold, a female answered the call. She began to say horrible things to me and proceeded to inform me that Donnie was her boyfriend and had been for the past 4 months. I was puzzled and could not believe what I was hearing. I instantly hung up with her and immediately dialed Donnie's number. Once he answered, I spilled out all the information I had just learned. In his response, he pretended to be clueless and stated that he had no idea what I was talking about.

Now I understood why he ignored me the whole trip. He was with another woman. I could not believe what was happening and had a horrible rest of the day at work. Once I arrived home, I noticed his car in the parking lot where we lived. Usually, he would be at work, and I was confused that he was home, but I decided that I would give him a piece of my mind. I entered our home and let him have it. We fussed and argued until I resolved that he had to leave and that I could not be with him anymore.

Soon he moved out and I found myself alone and full of sadness. I felt as if I fell into a depression. I only had the energy to go to work, come home, and sleep. I did not want to face the reality that I was alone and that it was finally over, so sleeping would make me forget about it for a while. I had many thoughts going through my head at this point and could not figure out how he could do such awful things to me. He not only lied and cheated on me, but he manipulated money out of me as well. How low could you be to ask your current girlfriend for $200 to spend with your new girlfriend? I felt so disgusted and could not imagine doing anyone like that.

After being cheated on for the last time in 2018, I thought I had enough! I wanted out and I needed to begin my healing process, but I still felt empty without Donnie. With me still being so in love with him, I continued to stay even though we were not a couple anymore. This allowed Donnie to still dib and dab with me, but still do his own thing at the same time. I knew exactly what he was doing, but I stayed in it because it was comfortable, and my confidence was very low. I did not think I could find anything better than what we had together.

I shamefully allowed this situationship to go on for another year. Even though we were not together or held any titles, I still had hope that things would get back to where they used to be. I just knew he would eventually see my value and marry me. I was wrong, so wrong! Donnie was continuing to enjoy this while I was being taken on an emotional rollercoaster. I was depending on him for happiness instead of finding it within myself. I was not focusing on God like I knew I should and I continued to idolize Donnie and prioritize him in my life.

In Fall 2019, Donnie and I talked about giving it another try of being in a relationship with a title. While I was so happy to get back together, it just still did not feel genuine. I was ignoring all the bad vibes and was so eager to enter back into a relationship with him just to feel complete again. Once we were back together for about a month, he told me there would be a possibility of him moving away to Texas due to a new opportunity that came up at work. In my mind, I wondered what would happen to us. I became very emotional because I felt that things were finally coming together for us.

After weeks of me asking about him moving out of town, I began to realize that maybe this was his way out of the relationship. Once I discovered that this was his attempt to escape, I became furious. At this point, I was completely fed up. I was so over the relationship and so over him! I willed up the courage to tell him that he would NOT continue to dictate what goes on with us and informed him that if there would be a relationship in the future, it would be based on my decision and not just his. Even though I had no intentions of getting back together, I was finally putting my feelings first. That was the first time that I made a major decision on my own during the entire span of our relationship.

With me finally putting myself first, I felt so empowered. I began to cast all my troubles on God and allowed Him to figure out things for me. He gave me the word to start journaling because I needed to get my emotions out. I did not have Donnie to tell all my problems to, but God set it up to where I could give it all to Him. I began to pray more while journaling, which was therapeutic for me. I do not regret anything Donnie and I went through and I use it as a learning experience. Donnie is a great man overall, but he was not ready for a serious and committed relationship and neither was I. God allowed us to go through this relationship for a reason to learn all the lessons we needed to learn. I would not have changed anything about our relationship because it has allowed me to be the woman I am today. I have taken a vow to do things God's way the next time I decide to enter a relationship or marriage.

September 13, 2019

"Don't be afraid, for I am with you. Don't be discouraged, for I am your God. I will strengthen you and help you. I will hold you up with my victorious right hand." - Isaiah 41:10 (NLT)

Today was an ok day because here I am again, missing Donnie. Some days I feel ok, Lord, but on days like today, I feel really sad. Not only do I feel sad, but I also feel afraid of how my future will turn out. Will I eventually feel better? Lord, I come to you today to give me strength because I really need it right now. You are the only person I have been open to about my situation or how I have been truly feeling. As I write down and explain to you how I feel, tears are filling my eyes. You know how I truly feel, so I ask you right now, Lord, to uplift my spirit and allow me to feel better. I will admit that talking to you, spending time with you and reading your word allows me to feel better. Going through this tough time and this heartbreak will eventually give me the strength and build me up to become a stronger woman with the help of you, God. Everything I try to turn to for happiness (food, watching tv, social media, etc.) only lasts for so long, and I just need you to wrap your arms around me right now, Lord, to allow me to experience the true happiness you want me to have. So, Lord, I pray that you can help me at this challenging time and allow me to feel better in due time. Amen!

CHAPTER 2
MOLLY & I

Molly, once upon a time was "My Girl," which is what I use to call her. We met at work in 2014, at the same workplace where Donnie and I met. Molly and I had mutual friends at work, making it easy for us to become close so fast. She was also dating someone at our job who was a great friend of Donnie. So, with her boyfriend and Donnie being great friends, I felt Molly and I should be great friends too, right?

When I first met Molly, I noticed how sweet and nice she was to everyone. I was like the new girl at work, so I did not initially talk to many people because I was still getting to know everyone. After a few months, Donnie and I were together, I noticed how

Donnie began to develop his own friendships at work, so I began to develop my own as well.

Donnie became really cool with one guy, which was Molly's boyfriend. Donnie would tell me how cool he was with him and how we should all hang out sometimes and double date. As a woman, when we hear "Double Date," we instantly get excited! We all planned to hang out on New Year's Eve 2014, but plans did not go through, so we had our first double date in January 2015. Molly made reservations for us at this nice restaurant, and I was like, "This girl has taste!" As we were on our double date, I began to know Molly a little more. I noticed that we had a lot in common, and I felt that I was talking to myself as I spoke with her. We shared some of the same interests and liked some of the same nice things. With fashion being our most common interest, we were known as "bougie" to others. After that first double date, we hit it off as friends.

After months of getting to know each other, Molly and I began to hang out without our boyfriends involved. If I was not with Donnie, I was with Molly. Although Molly had other friends, I had other friends as well, but we were spending a lot of our time together. Things were going so well with our friendship, and things were even better to know that our boyfriends were good friends as well. As time went by, we began to take trips together and spend more time together. I honestly felt that Molly understood me so much because we understood each other's relationships with our boyfriends, or at least I thought we did.

Things began to turn when I noticed how Molly was such a private person. Donnie also noticed how private she was also, so I knew I was not alone. Now I am not saying being a private person is a bad thing, but if I was willing to tell her private things about myself or my relationship with her, I expected that she would do the same since we were "friends." Molly began to portray herself as this perfect person and that her relationship was also perfect. I would tell her problems and be transparent about Donnie and I and she would state to me that nothing was going on in her relationship. Little did she know, Donnie would always tell me things that were going on in her relationship that she would not tell me, and I knew that she was not being honest with me. I began to feel betrayed by Molly because I thought we would tell each other everything. This was when I noticed how our friendship was not as genuine as I thought.

One time, Molly was having issues in her relationship, and I made sure I dropped everything and was there for her. At this point, I was honestly surprised that Molly was being honest with me, which made me want to be there for her more. We would spend hours on the phone because I did not want her to feel as if she was alone. I wanted her to know that I was there for her and willing to help in any way.

Despite her being a private person, I wanted to be there just as I wanted a friend to do for me.

Being there for one another began to happen more often. If Donnie and I were having issues in our relationship, she was there for me and I appreciated her for that. I felt like we were getting to know each other more and now I learned why she was so closed off with me initially. Maybe Molly needed to warm up to me, trust me and fully let me in. As years went by, Molly and I continued to be good friends.

In 2017, things began to change with our friendship when we found out Donnie was cheating on me with someone at the workplace. When Molly and I first found out about the cheating rumors, we did not believe them because we knew that Donnie would not do such a thing with this person. But as time went by, I began to feel like Molly knew more than she was saying. I felt like she was withholding information from me and I could not understand why. With all the cheating speculations and drama going around at our job, this put a huge damper on our friendship. I felt that everyone knew something about my relationship that I did not know. I felt so alone again due to my relationship falling apart and now my friendship with Molly falling apart as well.

With so much drama going on at the job, I felt like I could not trust anyone, especially Donnie and Molly. These were the two closest people to me and I could not confide in them about how I was feeling. I idolized them both instead of giving my problems to God. I got to the point where I depended on them both for happiness instead of finding that within myself. I was getting so wrapped up in the drama at work and listening to the "he says, she says," that it was becoming very exhausting to me. I just wanted Molly to be there for me despite what others said.

Now at this point, I was dealing with so much drama that Donnie created at work. I felt like Molly was somewhat being there for me, but only half-heartedly... I was getting into arguments with the woman that Donnie was cheating with from work, and I was saying to myself, "This is not me!" Molly was getting involved in arguments with this woman as well due to Molly being associated with me. As a result of so much drama circulating at work, Donnie, Molly, and I were let go from the job. I honestly felt terrible that Molly had to be wrapped up in our drama because she did not deserve that. Once Molly was involved in the drama, she began to despise Donnie and vice versa.

With Donnie and Molly not getting along, I found myself being in the middle. It was like Molly had something on Donnie, but wouldn't say the whole truth. She began to look at Donnie and I like as one when I needed someone to be there just for me. All the feelings she was having towards Donnie, she projected them off on me. I felt like she was trying to cancel both Donnie and I as friends due to Donnie's wrongdoings. I could not understand why she was acting like this toward me, and this resulted in us not speaking for a whole year.

After about a year passing, which is now 2018, my 30th birthday was rolling around and I was so excited to celebrate. Even though Molly and I were not on the best terms, I still wanted to include her in my birthday festivities. While trying to invite and include her, she was snooty toward me. Whenever I would tell her about my birthday plans, she would always have something negative to say about them. At that moment, I felt that she was jealous because the attention was not fully on her. Now, I have been so supportive to this girl, especially when it came to her birthday, and I felt I was not getting the same treatment I have always given her. I instantly felt like if the attention was not fully on Molly, she would not be supportive.

I noticed how she would complain about anything regarding any plans I made. Once it was time to celebrate my birthday, of course, Molly showed up but was acting so condescending. She was acting like: "I'm better than everyone, and I really don't want to be here." While at my birthday event, she barely even talked to me, and I began to question, "Why did she even come?" I thought to myself, "How ruthless could you be to treat someone mean on their own birthday?" After all of this took place, I felt our friendship would never be the same and I honestly was ok with that.

In 2019, I tried reaching back out to Molly around her birthday. She was very receptive to us, trying to talk things out and resolve any issues we still had. After several attempts of us trying to meet up, we were not successful. When I tried to meet up with her one last time, she was disrespectful towards me due to the unsuccessful meet-ups, and I was left trying to understand why.

I really wanted us to meet because around this time, Donnie and I were breaking up for the last time, and I felt I had no one to talk to. Everything ended with Molly and I having a very nasty argument and saying very hurtful things to one another. I felt like this was the end for Donnie and I, and also, Molly and I at the same time. I had no one to turn to this time until I came to the realization to pray and journal. I honestly felt like God was setting everything up on purpose to allow me to depend on Him more. I honestly did not understand everything that was going on with Donnie, Molly, and I, but over time, God has allowed me to understand fully. Both situations were seasonal, and I don't regret going through either one. I had to go through those situations to get me to where I am today. The following journal entry expresses the way I was feeling due to Molly and I falling out.

September 4, 2019

"Never pay back evil with more evil. Do things in such a way that everyone can see you are honorable." - Romans 12:17 (NLT)

In today's verse, "Never pay back evil with more evil," I can honestly say that statement is much easier said than done. The reason I say this is because of the argument I just had with my friend Molly. Molly and I were really great friends once upon a time, but as of recently, things have changed between us and things are not quite the same anymore. I am trying to become closer to you Lord and trying to do what you would do in certain situations, but I can honestly say that people can take you there. I really tried to allow things between Molly and I to get better, and I was willing to let old things go! She did not want to do the same, so I let it go! I am trying to be a better person and let old ways go, but if someone doesn't acknowledge that then I must give it to you God, which I did. "Do not be conquered by evil, but conquer evil with good." This quote speaks a lot, and I will try my hardest to do what this quote is saying with your help. So overall, Lord I pray that you continue to give strength and wisdom to not allow what others do to me to provoke me to retaliate or get even and hurt them back. But instead, I allow you to fight my battles and not feel like I have to handle everything on my own.

CHAPTER 3
ME, MYSELF, & I

PUTTING MYSELF FIRST

In the fall of 2019, I found myself alone. At this time, I was walking away from a 5-year toxic relationship and leaving a friendship that I thought was genuine. I felt like I tried my hardest to make both situations work, but neither Donnie nor Molly were receptive to it. I could not find it in me to beg anyone to be with me or to be my friend, so I had to walk away. Once I saw that it was so easy for them to walk away from me, I felt I had to do the same. Obviously, neither relationship nor friendship was meant to be because it should not be this hard. Walking away from both was the best decision I made, and I will explain why.

Throughout this whole process of putting myself first, I learned that you must love yourself before trying to love anyone else. Once you can fully be whole and love yourself, you will be able to properly love someone else, whether that is in a relationship or friendship. I was so focused on making Donnie and Molly happy that I was excluding my own feelings. I thought I could fix everything in both situations without them even trying to put forth the effort. With all the effort I was putting into mending both relationships with Donnie and Molly, I began putting it into building a better relationship with not only myself but with God.

Once I made up in my mind that I needed to put myself first, I began to get more involved with God. I was willing to let all the drama and past hurt go to start the healing process from both situations. I was praying and journaling more, which was very therapeutic for me. I found ways to get out any hurt or pain without expressing it to anyone. I could vent to God while He showed me new ways to release the pain. I was genuinely learning how to give it all to

God. Humans often mistakenly think that we have everything under control or that we can handle everything, but I am here to tell you we cannot. We must give all our burdens and problems to God so He can handle them accordingly.

When we cast all our problems over to God, He gives us the wisdom and knowledge to handle those problems. His way of thinking is much higher than ours and He teaches us to do it in a much easier way for us. It took me some time to realize that I could not solve everything on my own, but that is ok. I was so happy to finally do things God's way, and you can too, once you give it all over to Him.

I had to learn that I cannot depend on anyone for happiness. I had to take a vow to myself that I would not look for happiness in a man or a friend but in myself and God. True happiness came from building that relationship with God, and once I found it in Him, He gave me the word to pray more and to begin to journal. I started to have a new love for praying and journaling. Being able to release any hurt and pain by praying and journaling was such a blessing to me. Without me finding the connection with God and I, I would still be searching for happiness in someone else today.

Along with journaling, praying was another tool I used to help with my transformation. When I began praying more, I could unlock some of those blessings God had for me. Being able to put myself first was the ultimate blessing for me. I literally had to pray to God to teach me how to put myself first because, sadly, I did not know how. Once I was

> **Being able to put myself first was the ultimate blessing for me.**

able to put Alisha first, I began to recognize the actual value within myself. I also ceased to entertain anyone who could not recognize my true value as a woman.

Not only was I praying more, but I was also learning to pray properly, and I began to talk to God as if He were my friend and spend more time with Him.

Praying was a great outlet to tell exactly how I felt without anyone judging me. I felt like God was my own personal diary, and I could say to Him everything just as I did in my journal. Journaling and praying went hand in hand for me.

Before coming to Christ and being the saved woman I am today, I did not spend much time praying. I would pray every day, but just with a basic prayer. My basic prayer was to only pray for friends, family, and protection. Once I began to spend more time in prayer, it was like God and I was having a conversation. Not only was it like we were having a conversation, but it became routine for me also. Even though God does not speak back to me, we would have this dialogue between us. With talking to Him more, I would soon begin to hear God speak to me through different confirmations, dreams, or Him speaking through others. He would use others to give my answers. When I began to prioritize myself, I was able to gain my independence back.

Gaining my independence again was a huge accomplishment for me. I was so co-dependent on a man or friend that I forgot how to be independent. I know it sounds strange for a 30-year-old woman to be so dependent on others, but this is where I was in my life. I was determined to get back to me and grow to where God wanted me to be.

With gaining my independence, I found it exceedingly difficult to do things on my own, such as shopping. Shopping will always be near and dear to my heart, and when I found it difficult to shop, I knew something was wrong. With Donnie and I being so connected at the hip once upon a time, shopping was one of the many things we did together. Once we were no longer together, I began to develop separation anxiety. With overwhelming feelings of anxiety, I found it very hard even to shop, and I remember times when I would sit and cry in the car before entering a store or shopping mall. Once I found it difficult to leave my car before entering the stores, I knew that I had hit an incredibly low point. As time went on, with praying and depending on God more, shopping became easier and more pleasant. I can now shop with ease, and to be honest, I would rather do it alone.

At one point, I was so comfortable with being around others that I could not even imagine being alone. Living alone and being independent did not cross my mind until I had to do it. I was so consumed with the thought of being with Donnie forever I never thought that I would be single and independent. Now that I am a single and independent woman, I take so much pride in it. I now embrace my independence so much because I know what it took to get here and it has allowed me to grow into who I am today, which is the best I have ever felt. Going through what I went through with both situations has made me see myself for the woman I am. I now know I can be this independent woman and stand alone to fully develop into a woman of God.

For me to have gained so much confidence as a woman, I had to go through the process of becoming whole. After losing my support system, I was such a broken woman with a broken state of mind. In order for me to become what God needed me to be, I needed to surrender to Him to make me whole again. In my process of becoming whole, I was baptized in 2019, which allowed my transformation to begin. I began to experience many changes after being baptized, some of which I did not understand, and going through both situations was a prime example. Even though I did not understand some of those changes initially, I now see why they occurred.

I truly desired to become whole, and I was determined to learn as much as possible. I developed a hunger for reading and writing because I wanted to be the best version of Alisha that I could be. I know I needed to be whole to be ready for my next relationship or marriage. I felt like I made the mistake of jumping too quickly into my relationship with

Donnie and I did not know who I was at first. I needed this relationship with God to be considered whole before going into my next relationship with a man who is whole also. I am honored to do it in God's way this time around because I know it will be so blessed. Not only am I praying to be whole, but I am praying for my future husband as well so we can glorify God together.

Putting myself first was indeed a process that I had to go through. I had to learn how to stand alone so that God and I can have a chance to develop that intimate relationship that we have today. With also putting myself first, I had to do a lot of forgiving. I had to forgive those who hurt me for me and not for them. I had to move on and the only way I could do it was by forgiving them. Even though Donnie, Molly, and I are not on speaking terms today, I have no hatred towards them and I actually thank them for allowing me to become closer to God. I honestly feel God used them for me to develop a stronger relationship with Him.

I do not regret anything that occurred with us but more so embrace it because I would not be who I am today without it. It is such a freeing feeling to know I can let all the hurt go and now focus on what God has for me. I can finally say that I am doing it in God's way and putting myself first. I encourage you today to put yourself first for a change and channel in on what God has for you. Become that woman of God you are destined to become and allow Him to handle the rest. I promise you. It will bring so much fulfillment and joy in being who God wants you to be!

September 12, 2019

"A gentle answer turns away anger, but a harsh word stirs up wrath." - Proverbs 15:1 (HCSB)

I try to apply this verse to my everyday life because I feel there's really no point in making matters worse, but to try to solve every conflict positively. After dealing with my situations with Donnie and Molly, I feel there is no need to try to continue to confuse the situations but instead give them to you, Lord. I will admit, being in the situation, I was initially very angry. But today, I can say I am so glad I decided to stop trying to handle or solve every conflict and allow you to intervene because You can handle any situation better than I can. I decided to walk away from both situations because the battle is not mine, but for you, Lord, to solve. I am still hurt and sad about what happened, but maybe it's time to let it all go. I don't fully understand what you are doing, Lord, but I know I will understand in due time. So, in the meantime, Lord, I will continue to praise you, pray and allow you to solve every problem I may have. I just pray, Lord, you continue to let me be ok, and I thank you for allowing me to feel better. Amen!

CHAPTER 4:

MY SINGLE SEASON

EMBRACING THE PRESENT MOMENT

When you think of being single, what do you think of? Well, around the time I became single for good in 2019, there were so many horrible things I could think of as it pertained to being single. Lonely, sad, bored, being single forever were just a few thoughts that came to mind. I felt like there was no hope for me because it seemed as if all my previous relationships had ended so badly. I felt like I was being punished due to my previous relationships with men not working out. I began to question myself with questions like, is it me? Am I the reason for all my failed relationships?

At the age of 30, now single with no children, doubt began to set in. I began to question a lot, such as, "Why am I single?" and "Why haven't I had children yet?" I began to notice many of my peers either having children, working on more children, or getting married. Friends or family members would question me like, "Why don't you have any kids yet?" or "When are you getting married?" With all those questions being thrown at me left and right, I could not answer any of them at that time. With everyone questioning me, I started to question God. I felt I had no choice but to give it all to God and allow Him to handle the rest.

Transitioning to my single season was a little scary and lonely for me. I was now living alone, which was like the first time living by myself. Before moving in and living with Donnie, I lived with my parents, so I never lived alone until now. Initially living by myself, I disliked it so much. I felt all I did was go to work and come home to be lonely. During this transitional period, I found it so hard because in the past I was always accompanied by someone if that was with Donnie or with a friend. I was forced to grow into this woman of God that God wanted me to be without my permission. God knew I would not do it willingly, so He allowed what was happening to take place so He could take me to the next level.

With all these changes happening around me, I could not wrap my mind around any of them. There was still a lot that I did not understand, and I didn't know why God would allow me to feel this way. I wanted all the changes to stop, not knowing I had to go through this season to grow through it. Everything I was going through prepared me for what I had prayed for. We often make the mistake of thinking that everything we pray for will happen overnight, but this is certainly not true. We may have to go through uncomfortable situations to get to that thing we have prayed for. There is always a lesson or something God wants us to learn before receiving those blessings He wants us to have.

The most important piece of advice that I would like to give you is to continue having faith and praying when things are uncomfortable for you. This would be the perfect time to lean more on God and give it all to Him when going through an uncomfortable situation. Allowing God to handle your situation is much better than thinking you have everything under control. "With surrendering to Him, God met me exactly where I was in my life."

I had to get on the same page with Him, so I could finally experience the life He wanted me to have, and that was certainly not me being single forever. I began to stand more in faith for my future husband and children instead of questioning God why it hasn't happened for me yet. I stopped becoming angry and bitter when others would question me on things that I

> " With surrendering to Him, God met me exactly where I was in my life. "

did not have the answer to. I also began to manifest more of what I wanted out of life versus questioning or asking God. I began to believe that if I had the desire for marriage and children, God had those same desires for me as well. I knew I could not sit in my sorrow and feel as if I were being punished but tried to do whatever I could to turn my situation around with the help of God.

I was now at a place where I began to accept my singleness and embrace it at the same time. I also understood why I needed to have this single season to fully prepare me for what I have been manifesting. At this time, I started to have a whole different outlook on being single. I stopped looking at being single as a bad thing but as a brief time in my life to be whole and heal from any hurt I endured. I had more confidence that I would not be single forever, so I started to look at singleness differently. If I had known it would have felt this good to be single, I would have been more eager to walk into my single season earlier.

I learned to protect my peace by becoming more cautious of who I allowed in my space and being aware of unwanted energies. I now use my place as a sanctuary for God and I to become closer and to continue to develop our intimate relationship. God set it up for me to be secluded or separated from others to fully get my attention so I could finally focus on what He wanted me to focus on. I started to see the changes in myself while being single. I began to understand exactly what God was doing.

Cooking became more enjoyable again for me while alone, along with shopping. I was eager to find recipes to accompany my lifestyle as a single woman. Cooking and shopping were just a couple of interests that became more intriguing as I found myself. I was so proud to know that as a single woman of God, I was striving and moving the way God wanted me to.

When I feared being single, I was not fully trusting God after my breakup. Now that I am trusting God more and more every day, I have less anxiety about how my life will turn out when it comes to a relationship or marriage. I take more pride in being single, and I honestly enjoy it because I know that this is where God wants me to be in this season. Once you accept your singleness and begin to embrace it, it will allow God to know that you are ready to prepare for your next level. God wants what is best for us, and He does not want us to be stagnant but to continue to level up. So, the more you complain and avoid singleness, the longer you withhold what God has for you. I encourage you today to be happy where you are and to be hopeful for what is to come.

As I continued to embrace my singleness, I began to educate myself by researching ways to be successful in my single season. I began listening to Life Coach Sarita A. Foxworth as she gave women insight on how to thrive in their single season. I started following Sarita on Instagram in 2018 when I purchased her very first book, "How to Heal a Broken Heart", which is a great read, by the way! When I initially bought the book, I was experiencing my very first breakup with Donnie, and I wanted to receive any help I could. I was determined to get over the hurt of the relationship, not knowing that it would turn into this off again, on-again relationship.

Even though I was ready to heal from the break up, I still was not ready to break things off with Donnie for good. Sadly, I sat the book down for two years after only reading half of the book. At this point in 2018, I still had high hopes for our relationship and resisted that it needed to end. I was sure I wanted to start the healing process, but I still wanted to be with Donnie at the same time.

Fast-forward to 2020. I picked back up "How to Heal a Broken Heart" again. At this point, I was in a space where I was more receptive to receiving any tools that may be helpful to me while going through my transitional phase. Mind you, I was already somewhat going through the healing process by myself in 2019 when I began my praying and journaling journey. Once I came to the end of the book, I noticed how Sarita shared tools that she used to overcome her breakup and journaling was one of them. I was so amazed at what she shared because I did exactly what worked for her. God gave me the mind to journal, so once I finished the book and read Sarita's success story, that was all the confirmation I needed. The following journal entry explains my amazement on the day I finally finished the book.

March 3, 2020

Today, I have experienced confirmations over my life. I am so grateful for the journey You have for me and the progress of the road you have me traveling down, Lord. After finally finishing "How to Heal a Broken Heart", I learned that I have experienced those very same heartbreaks that Sarita has experienced. When starting the book two years ago, I did not finish reading due to trying to make things work with Donnie. I became so discouraged and unmotivated to finish the book that I sat it down for two years. Recently, I decided to pick back up the book, and I finally finished it today. Yay! When reading today, I received confirmation that this was all in your plan, God! Those very same things, such as writing or journaling, have helped Sarita heal and me as well. I didn't know that writing out your feelings would be so helpful to her as it was for me until today. God, you have helped me write out my feelings and hurtful moments just as you did for her. That is so amazing to me because I didn't know she would mention that, and I have already used journaling to help me. That right there was confirmation that I had done the right thing and needed to do it. Initially, I did not know that writing would lead to my breakthrough, but it has helped me tremendously! So, Lord, I thank you for the blessing and deliverance. Love you, Amen!

During my single season, another great book I discovered is "*Relationship Goals*" by Pastor Michael Todd. I was introduced to this book by a good coworker/ friend of mine, Victoria. I had seen the book circulate on Instagram, and I knew it would be a great read but never purchased it. Since I was noticing the book so much, I knew God was trying to tell me to read the book. While at work, I noticed Victoria had the book sitting on her desk, and I asked about it. She told me a little about Pastor Michael Todd and how she began reading the book. At this point, I was sold and knew I had to get my hands on it, so I purchased it that day. We began to read the book together. God sure knows how to use people to get us to do what He wants us to do! Prior to Victoria and I reading "Relationship Goals", we did not talk much, but now we are so connected, all thanks to God and the book.

CHAPTER 5

TRUSTING AND BELIEVING

While continuing to heal in my single season, I started to pick up more attributes that were important to me, such as trusting and believing. I began picking up these attributes once I grew faith in God. Trusting God with my desires, such as marriage and children, and leaving matters in His hands became more comfortable for me. I realized that I do not have to be fearful of how my life will turn out, but trust that God will make it His best.

I believe that trusting and believing is the first step when wanting to obtain the desires of your heart. Once you set in your mind what you want to obtain or accomplish, having faith should go along with it. What good is it to have a vision or dream if you cannot believe it or see it for yourself? Only you have the power to believe in yourself and trust that God will give you those desires of your heart. Once I could believe in myself and want different when it came to a relationship, changes began to happen for the better. I had to make up my mind and take on the responsibility of wanting that change. I could not depend on anyone to make those changes happen for me but more so, to make them happen for myself. I am pleased today to say that I wanted different for my life, and it all started with trusting and believing.

As of today, I continue to stand in faith for the desires of my heart, such as marriage and children. Even though I have not received those desires yet, I continue to trust and believe that it will happen for me eventually. When I give God my desires, I am aware it will not be given to me in my time but in His timing, which is perfect. If we were able to receive everything we wanted when we wanted it, then we would not know how to handle it. God is so strategic when giving us what we need when we need it. Just as I expressed in chapter 4, I had to go through certain situations to fully prepare myself for the desires I had been praying for. God does not always give us what we want when we want it because we would not be mentally ready for it. There is obviously something God wants us to learn or do to be fully equipped for His absolute best. I continue to patiently wait for those desires and not be discouraged while waiting, and I am also happy to know that no one or anything can stand in the way of what God has for me.

I felt that it was especially important for me to make my desires known to God when I was going through my transitional period. Even though God knows our desires before we are born, I feel it's so significant to be able to vocalize them to Him. God wants us to say out of our mouths our desires and why they are so important to us. Being able to express to

Him what we desire allows Him to know that we can trust Him and know that He will allow it to come to pass.

When I became single, I took a vow to date differently to properly prepare myself for marriage. I wanted dating to look different for me because I did not want to make some of those same mistakes from my previous relationship with Donnie. I now know my value as a woman of God, and I refuse to settle for anything other than God's best. I now know my worth and all I bring to the table. With me now knowing these things, I can now date properly and with a purpose. Dating with a purpose means that dating/courting leading to marriage. So, when dating, moving forward, I will not be consumed with the thought of waiting 5+ years to allow a man to know if I am wifey material. I can now discern if a man can recognize my worth and value in a purposeful relationship and marriage.

After enduring what I went through in my previous relationship, I now trust God because I want a different outcome. Initially, it was not easy because my faith was not set up the way it is set up today. As I continued to grow closer and closer to God, that's when my faith grew stronger also. And as I grew closer to God, while having faith, I became a more patient woman. I can now wait on God patiently to obtain His best for me.

Now, there may be times when we don't get exactly what we stand in faith for and that's ok. I want to encourage you that what we think is best for us is not always God's best. God wants the very best for us, and sometimes we tend not to understand because we are so focused on the no He has given us. If you can look at the bigger picture of it all, then you would know God just wants to protect us. I allow God to know that I want whatever He has for me in His will. My goal is for my desires and God's will for my life to align to receive those blessings that are meant for me.

To encourage you, even more, receiving a no does not necessarily mean that it will never happen for you. Maybe you need to be a little more patient due to more growth that may be needed. Just strive for God's best and you will always come out on top!

Trusting God with all my desires has allowed me to be more hopeful of how my life would turn out according to His will. God knew the life He had set for me, and all I had to do was get on board with Him. To be able to trust and believe was only the beginning of the foundation God was laying for me. "For I know the plans I have for you," says the Lord. "They are plans for good and not for disaster, to give you a future and a hope."-Jeremiah 29:11 NLT. According to Jeremiah, God already knows the plans for us. He wants us to believe that He will allow them to come to

> **To be able to trust and believe was only the beginning of the foundation God was laying for me.**

pass. Show God you are ready to receive those desires of your heart by simply trusting and believing.

September 18, 2019

"Take delight in the Lord, and He will give you your heart's desire." - Psalm 37:4 (NLT)

What I take from today's verse is to follow the Lord and He will give you your heart's desires. As of lately, I have been making my desires known to God. God knows my heart and my desires for my life. God knows I have the desire to be married and to have children. Things are just not adding up in my relationship with Donnie, and we are obviously confused about a lot. God, I know you are not the author of confusion but a creator of love! I am so thankful to know that whatever you have for me is for me and you will not allow me to be confused. I know things will not happen on my time, but in due time they will happen on your time. I am so over and tired of trying to figure things out on my time and I allow it to happen your way, Lord. Whatever you want me to have, Lord, you will allow me to have it and no one (no one) can take that away from me. So, Lord, I just pray you to continue to give me the strength to get through this tough time. If it is in your will, to have Donnie and I together, we will be together. But if not, I am ok with whatever decision you make for me. So, in conclusion, you know what is best for me and what my heart desires. I thank you in advance for whatever decision you make for me. Love you, Lord. Amen!

CHAPTER 6
HAVING PATIENCE

Patience: the act of having the capacity to endure what is difficult or disagreeable without complaining (Meriam Webster Dictionary).

Since I began focusing more on God, patience became more part of my life. I knew that if I wanted God to do something significant for me, I had to be willing to be patient with Him. In 2019, I was so desperate for any good changes God was allowing me to have that I would do any and everything He needed me to do. So, if that meant being patient for His best, I was willing to do it.

I would often hear others say, "God is always so patient with me," but I never quite understood that until I recognized that He was being patient with me. Notice that I said, "until I recognized" that He was being patient with me. God always has and will always be patient with us. His patience with us does not begin when we finally realize it, but He has

> **When God secluded me from others, it allowed me to fully understand the true virtue of patience.**

been and will be the entire time. When God secluded me from others, it allowed me to fully understand the true virtue of patience. It was as if I was so open and vulnerable to learning new things when alone. I now know that God was stirring up a good thing in me to allow me to be as knowledgeable and as patient as I am today.

God has proven that He has not and will never leave my side. He is constantly there, waiting patiently until we come to our senses to properly allow Him to lead. To be transparent, I battled for a while with whether I was comfortable with allowing God to fully lead. I had to learn that I cannot handle everything on my own so surrendering to Him was the best decision I've ever made. Once I decided to surrender, God was right there waiting on me. When I finally realized that God had been waiting patiently for me, that was the moment when I knew his patience for me. He was there the entire time, never leaving my side.

Once I saw how patient God was with me, I knew I had to be patient with Him as well. It was only right for me to wait on Him and continue working on me while waiting on my desires. God does not rush to get things done for us, but more so, He allows things to happen in His perfect timing. Stop and think about it. Things are so much better when they are in God's perfect timing. When things are going according to His will, you can guarantee that things will align correctly and make

> **Things are so much better when they are in God's perfect timing.**

more sense. My motto is, "If it's not from God, I don't want it." I am willing to wait as long as I need to receive His very best. I encourage you to do the same today to experience the full potential of God.

Now that I have grown in patience, I can wait patiently for my desires. I now stand on God's word that He will give me the desires of my heart, such as a great career, marriage, and children. I can wait confidently, knowing He will give them to me while not feeling discouraged. Since I am waiting confidently, my single season is more pleasurable than my idea of singleness in the past. I can wait peacefully for what God will bless me with and not have to worry if it will happen or not. Also, when waiting, I can work on myself as a woman and allow God to use me as He used me to write this book. I just want to do whatever God wants me to do to be that much closer to His promises.

I became more understanding and patient once coming to the Lord. Patience was one of the many attributes I picked up while allowing God to lead. I'm not saying I have it all together because I don't. I have my days; we all have our days. I still struggle with certain things in my everyday life, but I am more capable of tackling problems due to God working on me. I can also encourage others, such as women, and tell them about my personal experiences. By encouraging other women while telling my own experiences, I can tell how picking up these different attributes, such as patience, allows me to be a better woman of God.

I want you to know that we all go through some of the same struggles, and allowing God to work on us can be greatly beneficial. He teaches us how to do things His way with less stress. I just love that I can count on Him to help solve my problems and wait patiently while He does it His way. To be patient while having faith is what God would like for us to have as one of the many principles for our lives. I no longer have to be anxious when solving things my way.

Neither do I have to try to rush God or feel as if I am trying to help Him out. I don't know why we think we can help God out while knowing He is God alone.

We tend to pray for certain things, and instead of waiting patiently, we try to put matters into our own hands. We try to speed up the process, knowing things don't happen on our time. The sooner we realize that God will and always will have everything under control, the better off we will be. Sometimes we think that the more we pray, the faster things will happen for us. I am here to tell you that this doesn't make God move on our time or any faster. There may be times when we may receive something that we have been standing in faith for sooner than we expect. When we receive it sooner, this means it has been approved by God and aligned with His will.

There is also no need for me to scheme or steal but wait for the things God has for me. God is the author of our stories, and He already has it written. So, have patience. While He is busy writing our stories, when we remain patient, God may want us to learn something in the meantime. While we are waiting, we are building endurance and strength all at the same time. We truly learn our best lessons in life while we are having patience and remaining in the faith.

We also often make the mistake of thinking that God does not hear us or is not listening when praying in actuality, He is. God is listening and willing to help the entire time. He wants to know if we trust Him like we say we do or have confidence in Him. Once we begin to see God move and resolve our issues, then He begins to build more faith for us. When we begin to build more faith, it allows us to trust God, even more, when future situations arise. So, when God is not moving when we expect Him to, this would be the perfect opportunity to remain still and allow Him to work. Not receiving answers in an appropriate time frame for us means God is so busy at work behind the scenes and we must allow Him time to work.

Based on personal experiences, I have received the best answers from God when I decided to be patient and wait on Him. I now know that when I am in an uncomfortable situation that God is so busy, I have nothing to worry about. It is as if, when I am at my most vulnerable state, I am open to learning any lesson given by God. I also feel I am more receptive and open to receiving that lesson due to a desperate need for change. I honestly thank God for patience today because He had to use certain situations to teach me lessons. When things don't go our way, we often think God is punishing us, but He is teaching us. So, I don't want you to feel discouraged when things may not go your way but look at the bigger picture of it all. Life is about lessons and learning from those lessons, which can be helpful to us in the future.

God does not speak to us naturally and since He doesn't, He gives us lessons and that is His way of communicating with us. I feel we need to be more open to learning when God is trying to speak to us.

To be able to pick up the quality of discernment was very life-changing for me. *Discernment: the quality of being able to grasp and comprehend what is obscured (Merriam-Webster Dictionary).* Since being able to use discernment in certain situations, I am able to understand and have the wisdom to make the best choices for me.

In order for me to gain discernment and wisdom, I had to humble myself. Humbling myself meant getting myself out of the way and allowing God to take over. I had to allow Him to use me, and this all began by simply praying and spending time with Him. When we can show God that we are ready for Him to lead, He does things for us that no one is capable of doing. Praying has not only allowed me to become closer to God but to be closer to myself and get to know myself better. It just really amazes me how praying and entertaining

> **Praying has not only allowed me to become closer to God but to be closer to myself and get to know myself better.**

humility have changed my life for the better. So, when you are feeling God is not listening, I encourage you to remain patient and pray more. When nothing seems to be working or moving, this would be the best opportunity to stay faithful and still.

Today, I want to motivate you to allow patience to be a larger part of your everyday lifestyle. While remaining patient, there are so many benefits that come along with it. You are fully able to see how God operates for you to be closer to your manifested blessings. You begin to develop a better relationship with Him and understand why He is so patient with us. Once you can see why God is so patient with us, you will be more eager to be patient with Him. To be patient and want those desires He has instilled in us, we will be able to wait with confidence instead of being discouraged or bitter when things don't seem to go our way.

Also, while remaining patient, you will be able to build endurance and strength. As you can see, patience is an overall great attribute to obtain, which comes along with other great qualities. While sharing my experiences, I pray that you too can choose to be a more patient person and wait on God. God knows what's best for us even when we feel we have everything under control. While remaining patient, God is teaching, and He is taking us to the next level. We may not understand at the moment due to being out of our comfort zones, but it will all work out in the end. I feel we receive the best answers from God once we humble ourselves and be still while He works everything out for us. So be the patient person God has called you to be to receive the best blessings from Him.

September 20, 2019

As I was driving today, I was just thinking about the goodness of God and how it is good to make all your request clear to Him. As of lately, I have been giving my request to God as I pray. Lord, you know my desires and I am confident that you will allow them to happen for me. I have the desire to be married, have children, start a business, and any other blessings you want me to have, Lord. I have had these desires for some time now and I am willing to be as patient as you need me to and if it is in your will to allow me to receive those blessings. Lord, I am ready to do things your way now because my way does not compare to what you have for me. In the past, I thought what I wanted for my life was the best, but now gaining the wisdom of you, Lord, I was mistaken. Lord, you know what is best for me, and I trust you with everything in me because I know that you have blessings with my name on them. So, Lord, as I remain patient, I will continue to thank you and follow you to learn more and more about your will. *I love you, and thank you, Lord, for always being there for me. Amen!*

CHAPTER 7

FAITH MOVING MOUNTAINS

Nothing is too big for my God, and I say this with confidence! I know He can do the unthinkable along with the impossible. I have grown to fully trust God over the past few years because I have been placed in situations where I have no choice but to trust Him. Going through certain situations in my life has allowed my faith to be set up the way it is and truly put my trust in God. He can do any and everything for us, but we first must have it set in our minds that He can do it. To have faith the size of a mustard seed, to grow and flourish into something wonderful is Amazing to me!

> **To have faith the size of a mustard seed, to grow and flourish into something wonderful is Amazing to me!**

Once upon a time, I sadly had the mindset that some things were too big for God and that He couldn't do it. It took God one good time for Him to show up and show out in a situation to make a believer out of me. He is so faithful and always keeps His promises. I no longer doubt my God because He can literally move mountains. We may think something is too unattainable or impossible, but, He has solutions for our problems that we did not know existed. His ways are much higher than our ways and His way of thinking is so much different from ours. I'm just so thankful that He can handle my problems much better than I can imagine.

One major component as it pertains to trusting God is stepping out on faith. At times, we must build up so much trust in God to where we find ourselves stepping out on faith. A prime example of me stepping out on faith was writing this book. When God told me to write a book in September 2020, I was a little unsure if I heard Him correctly. As time went on and through prayer, I most certainly heard God correctly about becoming an author. On November 18th, 2020, I began to write this book, *I AM HER*. I had no idea what I was doing, but I was just being obedient to what God was telling me to do. I literally stepped out on faith even though I did not know what the ending result would be.

"Faith is taking the first step even when you don't see the whole staircase." - Dr. Martin Luther King Jr. After reading this quote, I honestly understood the meaning behind it because it was truly how I felt. I felt like I just needed to start writing, which was the first step, even though I could not visualize the top of the staircase. God knew I was so afraid to step out on faith, but He also knew I trusted Him. God used me and walked me through it every step of the way. I'm here to tell you, you too can step out on faith even if you feel uncomfortable, and the ending results will be so beautiful.

Along with having faith, it requires us to be still and patient while waiting on God to do something for us. While waiting, the flesh will allow us to feel as if God doesn't hear us. Trust me, I know it's easier said than done to wait patiently when we feel God doesn't hear us, but also trust me that He is with us all along. I have been placed in certain situations where I felt all alone. I was praying and praying and nothing seemed to move. Then I would get a little discouraged because I may have felt praying wasn't working. Whenever I would get discouraged, I would pray even more, which would reverse my way of thinking to believe it's possible. I could not allow myself to get to a point where I felt God had left me because He is so worthy!

When you feel alone or as if God doesn't hear you, I honestly feel this is the best opportunity to draw in closer and pray more. God wants us to show Him we can trust Him despite the current circumstance/problem we may be

> **We have to know that God is with us all along when we feel all alone.**

facing. We have to know that God is with us all along when we feel all alone. Drawing closer to God shows Him that we need Him even more versus turning to other things we think will solve the issues. Just know when God is quiet, He is working overtime to help us, and all we have to do is let Him fight our battles.

We must have the faith that He can fight any battle of ours. I'm not perfect, and I have struggled with allowing God to fight my battles for me because I felt I could handle it better, sad to say. Just because good changes were not happening when I wanted them to, I thought God forgot about me or pushed me to the side. God had to teach me that just because it hasn't happened yet, doesn't mean it **I always say, "delay does not mean denial."** won't happen. I always say, "delay does not mean denial." So, I've learned to allow God to fight those battles because He does a way better job than I ever could. Plus, it's easier for us to allow Him to fight those battles. God doesn't want us to stress about anything or carry any burdens too heavy for us. So, He offers His help to us to show how faithful He is to us.

Sometimes our faith can be tested just to see how capable we are to trust and believe in God. We not only go through certain situations to help build our faith but to trust in God and know that He can do it. When going through a test, we must know we will be learning something from the whole situation and come out on top. In life, I feel we need these tests and trials to be better women. I have been placed in certain situations in my life that I did not initially understand, but once I was able to come out of it or pass the test, I was able to understand fully. Without those trials and those tests, I would not be the woman I am today, helping to spread the gospel to you.

So, when we are going through a test, it may seem as if it's impossible to pass it or get through it. In the midst of the pain, we must trust and have faith that God will get us through. We start to wonder how

God could allow us to be going through such pain, but we must look at the bigger picture, which is to allow us to grow. We tend to get so comfortable where we are, and in order for us to elevate to the next level, we sometimes need a little push. God knows we will stay right where we are in our comfort zones, so Him pushing us is His way of showing us how much He cares. We often forget that when we pray for certain things, God has to prepare us for them, so we can be ready when we receive them.

We must keep in mind that God will be with us in the midst of our uncomfortableness, and He will never leave our sides. He assures us that He is faithful by keeping His promises to us. As long as we continue to hold on to those promises that He keeps, it reassures us that everything will work out in the end. Personally, whenever I'm having a hard time or feeling uncomfortable, I constantly remind myself that God is faithful and that He can do it again. I have to stand on His promises despite the current circumstances I may be dealing with. Honestly, knowing what God is capable of doing gets me through. Holding on to those promises gives me strength because I know He wants what's best for me and that's not to remain in pain.

January 26, 2020,

"You don't have enough faith," Jesus told them. "I tell you the truth if you had faith even as small as a mustard seed, you could say to this mountain, 'Move from here to there,' and it would move. Nothing would be impossible." - Matthew 17:20 (NLT)

Because of my faith in you, Lord, nothing is impossible. I know you can do exceedingly and abundantly. If I continue to have faith, everything will work out in my favor. I thank you for today's verse, Lord, because I continuously hear the scripture about faith as the size of a mustard seed from others but never read it in the Bible until today. I know that if my faith is like the size of a mustard seed, it can grow and flourish into something wonderful. I have the faith that you, Lord, will allow my career and goals to come true and allow me to create a family of my own. I depend on you to allow that to happen. I thank you, Lord, for the goals you allow me to have, and I just pray that you can lead the way and allow me to receive what you have for me. I will continue to allow you to lead the way because I do not want to do anything without you or without your permission. So, Lord, I depend on you to allow everything to work in my favor that is in your will. Thank you, Lord. Love you. Amen.

CHAPTER 8

JOURNALING

Who knew I would write a book? Who knew I would turn my journal entries into a book? Who knew a dollar journal from Old Navy would have changed my life for the better? God knew! He knew exactly where I would be today and that's telling my story while spreading the gospel. I am so honored to be used by Him, so I can now inspire you and let you know I am just like you. You too can turn your pain into blessings by simply listening to God and allowing Him to use

> **Being obedient to God and having faith is the ultimate equation for success in anything you do.**

you. Being obedient to Him and having faith is the ultimate equation for success in anything you do.

So, to take you back to the beginning, it all began in early 2019 when I took a shopping visit to Old Navy. While entering the checkout line, I noticed some cute journals with flower designs. I love flowers because it reminds me of happiness, and at this point in my life, I could use any happiness I could get. After noticing the flowers, I also noticed the journals were only a dollar, so I proceeded to purchase the journal. At this point, I was not a writer, but I bought the journal because it was only a dollar, to be honest. After purchasing the journal, I allowed it to sit on my coffee table for almost a year until I made my very first journal entry on September 3, 2019.

When I first began to journal, I was not journaling with the intent of writing a book, but more so to feel better. I just wanted to get the pain out and God gave me the idea to journal out the pain between Donnie and I. Once I began to journal and read my

Bible every day, I started to feel a whole lot better. I found journaling to be extremely helpful and therapeutic for me. I was able to get all the hurt and pain out without having to tell anyone. I could pour all my heartache, growing pains, happiness, and healing into a dollar journal. Even though I paid a dollar for it, it is now priceless to me. I will cherish my very first journal forever, along with the thought of journaling.

Journaling has literally changed my life for the better. It has allowed me to learn myself better and grow from any pain that I may have experienced at that moment. It has also allowed me to cope with pain when I felt uncomfortable expressing my pain to others. I'm so glad and honored to have allowed God to give me the gift of journaling. To think about my very first journal entry, I was in so much pain and in desperate need of God to help and heal me. Based on the first scripture used in my first journal entry, *"Trust in the Lord with all your heart, and do not rely on your own understanding; think about Him in all your ways, and He will guide you on the right paths."Proverbs 3:5-6 Holman Christian Standard Bible,* I was in need of some direction and help from God. This scripture was so perfect for the beginning of my journal because it has paved the way for me.

I was now finally open to receiving help from God about my breakup. So, my first journal entry was an invitation for God to intervene. In my first journal entry, I explained the connection between my experience at church that previous Sunday to Proverbs 3:5-6 and how it all tied together. I feel that I was meant to journal about that scripture because it allowed me to set the tone for the rest of the journal entries. God knew I could not lean on my own understanding and that I needed some sort of guidance. He then used my Pastor to tell me I was on the right path, which is what the scripture was stating also. I now look at my very first journal entry when heading down the right path, even though it definitely did not feel like it at the time.

Sometimes we may not feel like we are on the right track or headed in the right direction due to our current circumstances. That is why it is very important not to go off our own understanding. Just as I did not know where journaling would get me, I did it anyway to get the pain out. It's so imperative that we trust God with any plans that we do have. God will give us an idea or plan and He will handle the rest and allow us to be successful. I am glad I was able to trust God with the plans for my journaling journey that eventually turned into a book to be helpful to the next woman. Now you can begin your journaling journey and hopefully turn it into something wonderful, such as a book.

You can transform your life by simply journaling, so you can witness the changes your own life as well. One of the beautiful things about journaling is witnessing the changes in your life. When starting a journal, it is important to be very honest about what you may be dealing with. As you continue to write and finish your journal, you will notice the changes in your life, which can be very helpful and therapeutic. I just love that I can go back and reflect upon the changes I was able to experience. A part of growing and changing is to notice how you got to that point. Once you are able to see the progression within yourself, you begin to see the strength within yourself also. Those obstacles you thought you could not overcome are now defeated, and you now have it written on paper to prove it.

I often tell women who I encourage to journal always, always put the date on each journal entry. When putting the date on your journal entries, you are now able to keep track of your journaling journey and also your life's progression. Also putting the date can prove how quickly you can overcome certain situations in your life. When we are going through a painful situation in our lives, it can feel as if we are in the pain forever. But once we can write down our pain instead, we will now go through the pain rather quickly.

Journaling will also give you the strength and endurance to get through once you notice the good changes.

Once I began to notice the progression in my life through my journal entries, I noticed the same while writing this book. While writing this book, I noticed how strategic God was through my writings. God was able to give me the idea to attach a journal entry to the end of every written chapter. It was as if God had planned my book perfectly because my book goes in the same chronological order as my journal entries. When I finished my very first journal, I said to myself, "I can write a book." Then it all came to me that God had set this up all along without me noticing.

When it became real to write a book, I would begin to get random ideas about planning and structuring my book. I knew it was all God because it was easy and planned out so perfectly. To be honest, I couldn't come up with these ideas myself. God knew to use me to write this book to help others, and I knew

I wanted to be as obedient as possible. Before even writing my book, I knew I needed a format or outline to give me a sense of structure. So, I began brainstorming chapter titles and God helped me with this section as well. With my brainstorming, I often would jot down ideas that I would get throughout the day. It was as if God was dropping ideas in my spirit throughout the day to where everything began to add up and make more sense.

When it came to producing this book title, *I AM HER*, it wasn't the easiest. I wanted something to represent me and represent other women who could relate to me. After brainstorming and praying a lot for a title, I started to develop some ideas but wasn't quite there. I first came up with ideas like "I Am Like You," "I Am You," or "My Single Season," but these were not doing it for me. So, with trying to come up with something, I got *I AM HER*. Once I said it and wrote it down, I said, "This is it!" I was so honored to have God help me come up with this book title because I didn't get the idea from anyone else or mimic anyone. God knew to give me this book title because He wanted it to be something that came from Him and no one else.

As I stated earlier in the book, I want you to know that I am just like you. I was in your position at one point or could be right where you are now. It all began with one journal, one journal entry, and one idea from God that turned into a book. Journaling my pain has literally changed my life. If you can be obedient to God and live out your purpose, which He has destined for you to fulfill, you will witness His works also. God just wants to use us, and He used me through my writings. Just asking God what your purpose is will soon be revealed to you once you continue to have faith.

> " It all began with one journal, one journal entry, and one idea from God that turned into a book. "

In this conclusion, I really wanted to include how this was my favorite chapter to write. I was so excited to write about journaling because I wanted you all to know where it all began. I wanted to tell you about my journey and how it was all divine planning brought by God. I am truly a witness to what God can do for us once we trust, believe, and be obedient. If we can keep Him first and allow Him to direct our paths, He can do more than we can imagine. At one point, I wasn't sure what my purpose was, and I knew I wanted to do more beyond my college degree, so I began to pray and ask God to reveal my purpose to me. Sounds simple, doesn't it? But it's just that simple. I knew in my mind that if I ask, I shall receive, and nothing is impossible for God.

While waiting for my purpose to be revealed to me, God was setting it all up for me before even asking and before finishing my very first journal. I owe it all

> I am truly a witness to what God can do for us once we trust, believe, and be obedient.

to Him, and I am ecstatic with the continuation of glorifying Him and giving Him all the praise through my writings. I am proud to be an author today to spread the gospel and help connect others to God. I cannot express enough how journaling has changed my life and how beneficial it has been to me in my time of pain. To see how my pain transformed into blessings is still amazing and mind-blowing to me, and God made it all possible. I am so thankful for the purpose He has set for me.

May 15, 2020

After reflecting on my previous journal writings, I was able to read a journal entry from eight months ago (September 3, 2019). When I wrote that journal entry, I was so down and out and sad from my breakup. But today, Lord, I want to say that I feel so, so better. Thank you, Lord! During this time, I had just started journaling, and I am so glad that you gave me the wisdom to journal because it has been one of the best decisions I have made. I see how you have changed so much for me in just eight months, and I am excited to see what the next eight months will bring. I thank you, Lord, and give you all the glory for turning things around for me! I just get so proud of myself because I know where I was when I first started. I'm currently still single, but I am so ok with it because I know what you have for me, Lord, and the desires of my heart. I know that you will allow my husband to come to me and allow us to have children together. I don't get discouraged anymore because I remember those promises and know you will fulfill them. So, Lord, I am here to thank you over and over again because I know you are faithful! I manifest my handsome husband and our wonderful three children. And I thank you for my career. I know you will allow things to happen for me, so I thank you in advance, Lord. Amen!

CHAPTER 9
PRAYER WORKS

Is prayer a key component in your life? If not, I can share my story and how prayer has changed my life in hopes of changing yours as well. It was only until I grew a great connection with God that I had the chance to experience the true wonders of prayer. Having a great tool, such as prayer, has truly changed my life for the better, along with journaling. Prayer and journaling goes hand in hand for me and now they are both essential for my life. I honestly do not know where I would be without the two. Having something so sacred to me, such as prayer, has allowed my relationship with God to be set up the way it is today. I have had the chance to be closer and closer to God by simply having a conversation with Him. It all began with me wanting better for my life and I allowed prayer to transform me into the woman of God I am today.

Through my prayer life, I learned the true value of patience, which I mentioned in earlier chapters. I began to understand how patient God is with us and how He is right by our side until we come to Him. While learning how patient He can be with us, I knew I had to be the same with Him. Prayer had not only taught me patience but changed my life as a woman overall. I began to learn myself as a woman, which allowed me to work on the many things that would hinder my relationship with God. I would recommend prayer to anyone open to experiencing the wonderful works of God and allowing Him to take us to places we can't take ourselves.

When having a conversation or dialogue with someone, we expect the other person to listen and respond, right? Well, when it comes to praying or

> **While learning how patient He can be with us, I knew I had to be the same with Him.**

talking to God, it's the same exact thing. Even though God is not physically here with us in the flesh, He is always listening to us, trust me! Sometimes we may often feel like God is not listening to us and often pray about the same thing repeatedly. Now, there is nothing wrong with praying until something comes to pass because I usually do this myself, but God hears us the first time. We often mistake God not responding when we want Him to for Him ignoring us. He is not ignoring us, but more so knows the solution before it happens.

I am a witness to the wonderful things God can do, so I know He listens to me. He will not only listen to me but also listen to you if you can trust and believe first. God can literally blow our minds if we trust Him to do it His way. Once you begin to trust Him with your prayers and desires, you will manifest the blessings God has for you, which helps build your faith. God knows exactly what would help build our faith, as long as we let our guards down and trust Him. I give

God all my desires because I trust Him that much to know He will give me more than what I ask for. Rest assured, God has it all covered and under control, and all we have to do is simply have a conversation with Him.

I would like to be very transparent and admit that my faith has not always been set up the way it is today. I've had times in my life when I felt God was not listening to me. Even though I felt as if He was not listening to me, little did I know God was there all along. And I know that it can be a little discouraging when what we pray for doesn't come or when we want it to come, but God has it all under control. I also get how it can allow you to feel as if you don't even want to pray in the first place, but I am here to tell you once you are consistent with God, He will truly bless you. We have to be able to trust the process,

> " God will meet us right where we are in our lives if we can meet Him there also. "

His process, and the plan He has for us despite what it looks like at the moment.

And I also get if you are not comfortable praying due to not praying often or maybe not having a relationship with God as of yet, but trust me, God understands. You will never have to feel embarrassed or ashamed to come to Him because remember, He is always waiting on us and knows our hearts. God will meet us right where we are in our lives if we can meet Him there also. Once we can show God that we are willing to open up to Him, He will truly honor our decisions and begin to move in our lives like never before. Just simply having a conversation is where it all starts with God while being open and honest with Him. Once I began to set aside time for God and spend time with Him, it became therapeutic.

It was as if I was having my own personal therapy session with God while releasing any hurt and pain I was dealing with at the time to Him. Because of my horrible breakup, I was able to develop a stronger relationship with God while using prayer as one of those tools to help me. Having prayer to help me along the way was one of the many things I used to help with my relationship with God and it has truly given me strength. Once I was able to see how prayer was so helpful during my breakup, I used prayer as my first option when dealing with any problem in my life, instead of a last option. I saw how fast God was able to turn that situation around, and it gave me more hope and, most importantly, more faith to know God can work anything out.

I had to go through those growing pains after dealing with the aftermath of my breakup with Donnie and losing Molly as a friend. Praying daily gave me what I needed as it pertained to a closer relationship with God. Without that relationship with God, I would not have known He was right by my side when feeling alone.

While going through the growing pains and storms, God made it His duty to turn it into something good for me.   Being consistent while praying has shown me that tough times do not last forever, and we go through storms for a reason. Sometimes God must remove certain people from our lives because they don't have permission to go with us to the next level. When people are removed from our lives, we may not understand it at the moment because we are so focused on the situation instead of what God may be trying to tell us. So, for us to grow, we have to be willing to do exactly what God has called us to do.

I know it can be very saddening when the person you thought you would marry and spend the rest of your life with is no longer there, but trust me it's for the better. With prayer and talking to God, He revealed to me that Donnie was not the one for me. With me hearing from God and all the signs there, I knew I had to listen to His instructions. When listening to God's instructions and being obedient, I knew this was the only way to be free from all the hurt and pain.

Also, listening to God's instructions has taught me what not to deal with today. I have gained so much discernment and wisdom from that relationship that I know what I will not tolerate as a woman. Going through those same growing pains has allowed me to learn what is from God and what may not be from Him.

While going through the pain, of course, it hurts, but today I honestly appreciate it because it has made me into a wiser woman of God. So, if you feel it is not from God, chances are it's not, and it's ok to let it go and trust that God has something much better for you. It will hurt initially but trust me, you will feel so good allowing God to lead the way. By trusting God, you will know when something is for you instead of going off your own understanding.

When I first made the choice to walk away from my previous relationship and friendship with Donne and Molly, I felt so depleted. I felt like I wasn't making the right choice, but God soon reminded me that I was. He gave me ways to replenish or restore myself with strength, and prayer was one of them. Along with praying, He allowed other like-minded people like myself to show me how to obtain more strength. I was more encouraged to read my Bible correctly and fast to gain more strength from God. I had already been journaling, so adding new ways to become closer to God was exactly what I needed at the time.

What I have learned over time with my relationship with God is just when you think you are the closest you could ever be with Him, there is always room to grow closer. He allows us to continue to grow and evolve, and I was properly able to do that while using those principles, such as praying, reading, writing, and fasting. I allowed praying to be the foundation between God and I because that's where it all started with us. I'm so thankful for our relationship and I wouldn't be the woman I am today without it. To have prayer

> **I allowed praying to be the foundation between God and I because that's where it all started with us.**

as the connecting piece between us is what I needed when I found myself lost and low on strength. He will give us exactly what we need as long as it glorifies Him.

Having a prayer life has tremendously impacted my life. I have allowed prayer to be a part of my daily routine to keep that intimate relationship between God and I going. I have grown so accustomed to spending time with God daily to where if I don't do it then everything is off for me. So, taking that time to spend it with God is so important to me because it is a decision I have made on my own and not for anyone else. I can honestly say I have decided to have this walk with Him, and for once in my life, I did not need a man or a friend to make that choice for me. I knew this was something I had to do for myself, and I will never let anyone get in between God and I.

I knew I needed to be consistent when having this time with God daily to experience the fullness of Him. With me incorporating journaling as a part of my daily routine along with praying, I thought, why not combine the two. So, I came up with the idea to have my own personal prayer journal. In this prayer journal, I would jot down things I wanted to pray about for the day or what I wanted God to do for me at that time. I began to pray not only for myself daily but also intercede on the behalf of others as well. I feel like God was able to place me in a position to pray for others and my prayer journal was the perfect place for it.

Not only was my prayer journal used to list things I wanted God to do for me and others, but to have a note section to journal about what I just prayed about that day or what I saw God doing for me and others in the future. And what's amazing about my prayer journal is to be able to go back and reflect on what I may have been standing in need of and seeing it come to pass. I am a witness to seeing how God works and I have a prayer journal to prove it. I would like to encourage as many people as possible to do what worked for me because if it could work for me, it would work for you as well.

Effective praying has been a big component in my life for the past few years due to me noticing the wonders it has done for me. Once you see that something is changing in your life for the better, you would not want to turn away from it either. Prayer has become so significant in my life due to its results. I now realize that God does listen to me, and I'm not just having a conversation with Him for nothing. He has been able to get me through hardships that life can throw at me, allow me to learn from them, and be willing to help another woman out like myself. He has also been able to restore me and give me the strength to get through anything when I felt I could not go on. Allow prayer to be the essential piece in your life to allow God to give you whatever your heart desires.

May 17, 2020

"The Lord who made the earth, the Lord who forms It to establish it, the Lord is His name, says this: call to me and I will answer you and tell you great and wondrous things you do not know."

- Jeremiah 33:2-3 (HCSB)

Today's scripture was sent to my phone for the daily scripture. I really enjoyed reading the devotion that I wanted to write tonight. God stated that if you "call to me, and I will answer you." I just pray, Lord, that you can direct my life in the direction you see it. I know I often try to plan my own life and not wait on you, but I need not do that. I want my life to go in the direction it should with the help of you, Lord. I like the statement in the devotion, "but unless you ask God to show you who you really are and let Him direct you along the journey that is meant to be your life, it won't happen." So, Lord, I am asking you, who am I really and what do you see me doing? You know the desires of my heart, so I know you will take that into consideration. I want to know the plans you have for me and know what I should be doing at this particular time. Just allow me to focus on myself more and allow you to lead the way. I put my trust in you, Lord, and I depend on you. Thank you, Lord, for the process. Amen!

CHAPTER 10

DOING IT GOD'S WAY

After many years of thinking I knew what was best for my life, I finally decided to start doing things God's way. I knew I had to make some major changes in order for me to live out the full potential of the life God had for me. I became open to the possibilities of having a better life by simply listening and following God. This does not mean that there were no times when I fell short, but He constantly reminded me where I belonged. I thank Him for the reassurance that I am doing it the right way.

> **" I became open to the possibilities of having a better life by simply listening and following God. "**

The first step in doing things God's way was for me to truly put Him first. I had to learn that for me to take this walk with God seriously, I had to follow Him and block out all distractions in my way. It was a process for me to understand that it doesn't work trying to do things my way and His way. To be honest, I still have my times where I may get distracted, but God always gets me back on track. I'm so thankful that I can constantly be reminded to stay on track because it can be so easy to fall back victim into the world. It's easy to be transformed by this world, and it can be difficult to get out, but with strength from God, we can. Once out of the world, it's best to stay out and be safe with God.

With me taking my walk with God more seriously every day, I knew I had to be for real with Him. I remember having a conversation with Him and saying, "I'm just watching you, Lord." I'm so focused on the things of God now, and I decided just to sit back and see what He does next in my life. I have gotten to the point where I'm done trying to figure things out for myself, so I would rather chill and trust God. It's so much easier when we can just sit back and watch God work because it takes the pressure off ourselves and helps us not to think that we have to have everything under control. Now, I can truly focus on the things He has for me, such as my purpose and my calling, while remaining focused on Him.

I had to make sure my path was clear when following God and allowing Him to order my footsteps. I could not allow a man to be a distraction when it came to my relationship with God again, so I was cautious about who I let in. I've learned so much from my relationship with Donnie and now I refuse to allow a man to get me down like that again or mess up what God and I have. I knew I needed a clear path to only see God's footsteps and no one else's steps. I can't allow anyone to mess up what

> " I knew I needed a clear path to only see God's footsteps and no one else's steps. "

God and I have, and I cannot get involved in any more ungodly soul ties. An ungodly soul tie is a connection with anyone who is known as a distraction in your life and interferes with your relationship with God. At this point, I knew I was ready to receive whatever God had for me based on the decisions I chose to make.

I had to start making better choices for my life because I didn't always make the wisest decisions. I knew I had to get a grip on my own life because I felt my life was headed in the wrong direction and that was away from God. I was so focused on the relationship between Donnie and I that I was neglecting the possibility of a better relationship with God. Of course, I was not attending church as I should because I would rather be under Donnie and watching his every move. I was so attached to this man that I was willing to tolerate almost anything he did to me. I became so dismissive of his cheating ways that if I found out anything he was doing, I was so willing to forgive him and take him back willingly.

I had such low esteem, and I believed he was the best I could get. I didn't properly love myself, and the consequence of that was remaining in a relationship I knew I should not have stayed in. With no proper relationship with God, it was impossible to love myself properly and the way I knew I should. God is love and in order to love myself properly, I knew I had to be more engaging with Him. Since having a better relationship with God, I can now love myself more and realize my worth. So, it came down to loving Donnie or loving myself, and of course, I chose myself while loving God.

Even though I neglected a relationship with God, He never threw me away, instead, He had mercy on my life. Despite the decisions and choices I made, He never gave up on me and I will forever be grateful for that. So, I took a vow that I would never give up on Him either, despite of what my current circumstances would tell me. He loves me so much that He was willing to pick me up right where I was because He saw something in me. He has chosen me and believes that I am worthy enough to do His work even when I didn't see it in myself. He has hand-selected me to be responsible to spread the gospel.

Since He cares for me and believes I can do His work, I couldn't continue to be so hard on myself. I had to realize that I am not perfect and that I am human at the end of the day. So, if God can have so much grace and mercy upon my life, I should be able to do the same thing, right? I had to understand the journey that I was being taken on and know that nothing would be perfect. I began to acknowledge that this walk with God is a process and that it's ok to have trial and error. There will be times when I would fall short, but if I can pick myself up with the help of God, I can keep striving for His best. Now I give myself grace and embrace wherever I'm at in my life, and I do not put too much on myself.

I can now trust the process better because I can trust God more. Just because things don't look the best initially doesn't mean they will always remain the same. Being in those situations with Donnie and Molly has shown me that God could turn situations around when we trust Him. Going through the process and trusting it, I learned that I am stronger than I think. I realized that I could get through this as long as I was consistent with God. It took me to have gone through both situations to know my own strength because I literally had to push my way through. Since I could get through, I now feel invincible and know I can get through any similar situation on top. I really didn't know how strong I was until I had to be strong.

Along with trusting the process with God and I, I had to be obedient to Him. I had to get to the point of knowing that He was removing both toxic situations from my life so He could get my full attention. I had to be willing to remove all distractions from my life to make room for all the blessings coming my way. When I was obedient and let those situations go, my relationship with God truly began. I could hear from Him clearly and be more in tune with Him. Of course, I didn't want to let those situations go, but now that I look back at that time of my life, I would have done it sooner to experience how I feel today.

To be honest, I don't know where I would be if I was not obedient to God and decided better for my life. I often sit and wonder, "Where would I be?" Then I think about God's grace over my life, and I don't want to imagine life without Him. I knew God had a calling on my life and that was to continue to spread the gospel. I often say to myself, "God is calling me higher." I just knew He would put me on a platform to tell everyone about Him, and I agreed to do so if He gave me the opportunity. It was like God was holding me accountable to tell everyone, especially women, so I knew I had to be obedient. I'm so glad He chose lil' 'ol me, and sometimes I can't believe He chose me, but I am so grateful!

The more obedient I found myself being, the more I found myself closer to God. I knew God would honor me for my obedience, so I did everything in my power to do it His way to make room for new changes.

During my walk with God and what I continue to learn today, is that no matter how close I think I am to Him, there is always room to become closer. Once I got saved, I mistakenly thought that was it. "Ok, I got saved, this is the closest God and I will ever be," is what I would often think. As I grew closer to God, I realized that this is a growing process, and I am constantly evolving. I'm happy to have those moments in my life where I received an extra boost closer to Him while removing something from my life that no longer serves me any more purpose.

There have been things that I have done in my life that I am not proud of, but removing those very things has allowed me to be one step closer to God. I got teary-eyed writing that last sentence because I know I am not perfect, and it definitely was a journey to being where I am today. I want you to know that you can do anything with God because He makes it all possible for us. Absolutely nothing is too big for Him, and He can fix any problem that you may have. You are hearing this from a woman who once upon a time thought God could not work it out, but has been proven wrong! I dare you to try Him, and I promise you that He will make it happen. I cherish my relationship with Him because He fills me up in ways I never thought He could.

I allow God to fill me up versus depending on a man, friends, or anyone to complete me. I constantly ask God, even today, to continue to allow me to be more self-sufficient on my own while depending on Him. I had to learn not to put all my trust in anyone because it only leads to disappointment. I honestly could not trust myself because there are times when I would fall short or don't make the wisest decisions. I sometimes cannot trust my own emotions or feelings as they can also lie to me, especially as it pertains to men. I needed God to fully equip me with the discernment to make those wiser decisions to know what is from Him and what is not.

Until I gave God permission to fill any void in my life, I sadly allowed inappropriate things or people to try to complete me. I recently just got to a point in my life where I realized I was leaning on the wrong things to fulfill me and I needed God to fill all the emptiness I was experiencing. I had to understand and get to the deep-rooted issues I was experiencing in my life to fully allow God in. I had to know I could not continue to use those inappropriate things to try to fill those voids for me because I was allowing myself to go in circles. Now I have to fully let God in to fill any void of mine, so He could fill it with all the wonderful blessings He has for me.

I have come to the conclusion that I want to do it God's way and I just want to be happy! I was committed to removing anything from my life that no longer served any purpose and that goes for today also. I now realize that it starts with God and I, versus depending on a man or friend. I can now be more independent and take a step back to evaluate any relationship and discern if it is for me or not. I now cherish my friends and family more who have been here for me all along, even when I felt alone. It's as if I'm more aware of the people who care for me and who don't want to hurt me.

My happiness today is essential to my life, and I can't allow anyone to take it from me again. I choose happiness every day while choosing God! I allow myself to do it God's way, which is the best way for me and for you as well. See, when we are determined to do it His way, He lays the foundation for us to be set up to receive all the blessings meant for us. I know for me it was a process to do it His way due to my own selfish ways, but I am now more open and acceptable to Him. I know God is not done with me yet, nor have I reached my highest potential with Him due to me constantly evolving.

So, today I choose God because He has already chosen me. Allow Him to pave the way for you and watch how He can literally blow your mind. From me initially questioning God if I really should write a book to where I am now is amazing to me. Sometimes I still can't believe how much He has changed the dynamic of my story and sent my life in a different direction. Once I was able to surrender and move out of the way, He showed me exactly where to go, and that's being an author. I'm so honored to do it His way because it is more than what I could have thought of for my own life. I will continue to strive for the best while encouraging women along the way.

June 7, 2020

Nine months later, after initially starting my journal process, I will say I am truly happy! Happy to be able to witness and see my growth through my writing, and also how I feel inside. I am genuinely happy, Lord, and I owe it all to you. To be able to experience this process throughout my life allows me to feel overjoyed. In this journal, I was able to let out my fears, tribulations, anxiety, my heartache, my manifested desires, and my love for you, Lord. To know that I trusted you along the way and to put all my faith in you, Lord. I'm forever grateful for you to allow me to start this journaling process and for you to lead the way. When starting the journal entries, I was in a place where I did not want to be but going through that situation has allowed me to be the woman I am today. Without going through the pain, I would not trust you as I do, Lord. I often hear people say how they would have so much faith in you and trust you so much, but I truly did not understand those statements until I experienced some of those things I wrote about in this journal. To be able to give you the desires of my heart when it comes to my relationship with you, Lord, my career/business, my future husband, and future children. I know you will work it all out for me according to your plan. So, in conclusion, Lord, I thank you for the journey and for allowing me to see my transformation within myself. Just because I am at the end of my journal does not mean you are done with me. So, as I enter my next journal and next chapter in my life, I continue to be hopeful that you have the best for me. I'm just so ecstatic to experience this journaling process and flourish into the woman you want me to be. Thank you, Lord, and I truly love you so much and can't thank you enough. Amen!

CONCLUSION

Now that you have heard my story, what do you think, Sis? I'm just so glad that I could bring you into my world and tell my side from my perspective. I hope I have helped you in a way to where you are now open to the possible changes God has to offer. I always state, "If I could touch one woman's life, I would be satisfied," but I know I will touch thousands. I feel so blessed to be put in a position by God to help spread the gospel to you. He is so awesome, and He can put us on platforms to tell everything about Him as it pertains to His goodness. I just hope my story can be an inspiration to you in the hopes of you becoming closer to God also.

Just as I stated in earlier chapters, I honestly did not know I would become an author until November

2020. I always knew God had something special for me, but not knowing I would become an author. I just knew I had to be obedient to Him and answer His calling of writing a book. Obviously, He saw something in me that I did not see in myself, and I promise He can do the same for you. I did not know the first thing about writing a book, but He surely showed me the way and used others to help me along the way. The decision to write a book was not mine, seeing that I went to college for a Social Work degree. But God knows what is best for us and all we must do is go along with His plans to live our best lives possible.

Now that I look back from the very beginning of journaling, God was dropping seeds. He was dropping seeds in hopes of flourishing into a beautiful flower. God knew my love for flowers, which attracted my attention to my very first

> **He was dropping seeds in hopes of flourishing into a beautiful flower.**

journal. The first time of purchasing my journal, He knew I needed some happiness in my life and that's exactly what journaling did for me. He set everything up perfectly for me, which led me to where I am now and that's presenting my first book to you. This is exactly where my love for sunflowers came about because having them brings me so much peace and happiness.

Of course, going through this journaling/writing journey has been very rewarding for me, but very challenging for me as well. Having to revisit my past from 2019 with Donnie and Molly was not easy for me. I found myself reliving those same moments that hurt me, which caused a little anxiety for me. I constantly asked God if I was making the right decision to write this book because I was so afraid of the backlash from others. After asking God numerous times, I concluded that I should not question God but trust Him more so. I realized if God gave me the idea to write the book, then He has everything under control and He has my back. I couldn't worry about what others would say but trust that my book would help someone, which is my purpose for writing it.

What we think is sent to destroy us, God will use it for our good and that's turning our pain into power. So, whatever may be causing you pain or hurting you today, God can turn that all around to allow you to be free and use it as a blessing for you or others. Even while writing my book, there were things or people sent my way to throw me off or to distract me, but of course, God rebuked them to allow me to finish. I never gave up because I knew God had a message for me to get out, so I knew I couldn't quit. I had to keep it going and continue to be obedient to receive all the blessings He has for me.

Writing this book has allowed me to do something pleasing to God, but yet passionate to me. I had to make the decision to be so open to whatever He had called me to do to live out this life He has for me. I know He is not finished with me yet, and I absolutely look forward to whatever He has in store for me. If you feel God is nudging or calling you to do something to glorify Him, I suggest you do it! Please do not sit on what He has for you because you are afraid. He will guide you and show you the way, trust me! God does everything with a purpose, so know it will all work out for your good. He can make anything possible for us as long as we can continue to trust and believe in Him. Just give Him a chance and it will all work out.

When it cames to writing this book, I don't take any credit for it. God gave me the mind and wisdom to make everything possible as it pertains to this book, and I will forever thank Him for that. He honestly gave me the idea of "I Am Her" and the purpose behind the title. I wanted this book to be very relatable to the like-minded woman to allow Her to know if I can do it, she can do

> " If God can turn my life around towards Him, He can most certainly do the same for you. "

it as well. If God can turn my life around towards Him, He can most certainly do the same for you. Now that I was able to teach the tools I used to have that closer relationship with God, I pray they can be useful for you as well.

Along my journey, God has made everything possible for me and He has allowed others to help me along the way. I would not be who I am today if it wasn't for God and the transformation of the mind that He has allowed me to have. I give God all the glory so please don't congratulate me, but more so, glorify Him. I am honestly just a vessel and I am the one of many being used to help spread the gospel. I am so honored to write this book and complete the work God has started in me. I pray for nothing but success for you regarding living out your purpose and doing exactly what you were called to do. I wish you nothing but the best, and just know there is truly no limit to God!

September 9, 2021

Today is the day I officially finished my book! Just a year ago, God gave me the mind to write a book, not knowing I would be completing it just a year later! I know this book will be very impactful for women across the world and that it will be just as impactful as it was for me to write it. I am just glad I could finish the work God has started in me to help someone. Who would have known this all would have been possible with just a $1 journal from Old Navy? God has allowed me to turn my pain into power by simply writing my feelings/emotions in a dollar journal. He knew I would be right where I am today and that's telling my story to the world in hopes of getting you on the path of truly learning what your purpose is. I just say I am so thankful for the process and the journey. I had to go through those hard and trying times to get to where I am today. I'm just thankful for the journey because it has truly built my character into the woman of God I am today. What was meant to destroy me has allowed *me to come out on top. I am so on fire for God and will continue to be. I made the decision to be a true follower of God and allow Him to take me where I need to go. I'm just so thankful for the process, progress, and continuing to do something pleasing to Him. Amen!*

ACKNOWLEDGMENTS

God: Lord, I thank you for placing me in the position to tell everything about you. I am so honored to do it your way and surrender to receive all you have in your will for me. I just thank you for being the leader in my life and showing me the direction I should go in. I also thank you for the wisdom and the knowledge to write this book to continue spreading the gospel.

Mom: Mom, I would not be the woman I am today without you setting a great example for me. You are truly the strongest woman I know! I thank you for teaching me how to be a woman of God by just simply watching you and you leading the way. You being the first woman I had the chance to look up to, molded me into who I am today. You paved the way for my childhood leading up to my adulthood.

Dad: Thank you for being the wisest man I know. It seems like you have the answer and solution to everything. You are always there to listen to me and give me the best advice ever. You are the true example of the man I seek in a future spouse. You have paved the way for me to know and understand what I deserved and how I should be treated as a woman. I will always be your Baby Girl.

Dominique: My sister and my friend. Someone I always looked up to and wanted to be like as a younger girl. You're always teaching me things without you even knowing. I have learned so much from you, you are a great example of a mother to Jaylun. I pray to be the best mom to my future children as you are to my nephew. You are such a Hard Worker, a Hustler, a Go-Getter and so determined to reach all your goals.

Matthew: Matt, thanks for being the best brother ever!!   You are so cool, laid back, and full of knowledge.   You continue to strive for better and continue to excel.   You are so open to learning new things and reading to broaden your understanding. You are the true definition of a Cool Dad and is always so patient with Zoe.   I'm so glad to have you as a brother to continue to learn from and to show me what a great father looks like.

Jaylun & Zoe: To my niece and nephew, I love you all so much and look at you all like my own children. You both are so smart and I hope my children can exemplify the qualities you all show. I pray you both can continue to grow into who God has called you to be and grow up to be true followers of God.

Pastor Morris Riddle: Pastor, I thank you for being like a second father to me. You are truly a great leader to the church of Harvest of Blessings Reconciliation

Ministry and continue to allow God to use you to help others. I can't thank you enough for your contribution to the process of me becoming the saved woman I am today and the process of my baptism. You are a true definition of a teacher.

First Lady Karen Riddle: Mrs. Riddle, I am so happy to have you in my life. I'm so honored to have someone like you who listens to me and would drop anything for me to say a powerful prayer just for me. I thank you for always believing in me and taking on the role as the First Lady of the church and meeting us right where we are and extending a hand. You are so caring and selfless and will always be a great helper.

Harvest of Blessing Reconciliation Ministries: A place where I call my church home. Where I can fellowship and praise with others to allow me to be closer to God. I was able to walk into this place a broken woman and was able to walk out as a healed, transformed Woman of God. I am thankful to have grown so much and continue to grow and learn as I pursue my relationship with God.

Whitney: My best friend of 20+ years, who knows me better than anyone. You are such a Boss and Businesswoman. I love the fact that you were brave enough to step out on faith and start your own business. You are a CEO and a motivator all in one. You have paved the way for other women to be strong enough to go for what they want and get that business. I just thank you, Whit, for giving the best advice and having such sharp discernment.

Allie: I love how once we met each other, we became instant friends. You have always been so mature and wise to me, and I always looked up to you to give me the best advice. You also are a great mother to look to for guidance as I continue to wait patiently for my future children. I just thank you for being there for me always and not allowing anything to interfere with us.

Barbara: I thank you, Barb, for always being such a real and loyal friend to me. I don't ever have to question your loyalty to me, and I can always trust you. You have always been so sweet to me and others and that will always get you far. You also show me how to be the best mother to my future children.

Bria: To Bria, my Meatball, my younger sister I never had. You remind me of myself so much and I truly can see myself in you. I am so honored to have someone like you to look up to me. You have always been so smart, and I hope you continue to grow and excel into the woman God wants you to be.

Sakari: My Iron Sharpens Iron Sister! I am so happy to have a friend like you, Kori, to grow and learn with as we continue to intercede for our future husbands. We are so similar and share some of those same desires we patiently allow God to manifest into our lives. I pray God continues to take you far as long as you continue to trust and believe.

Zoraida: To my Z, I cherish our friendship so much and I am so honored to call you my friend. I thank you for the book "The One Revealed" by Karolyne Roberts as a birthday gift in 2020. Reading that book has allowed me to get to know the author which led me to the publishing process of my book. I am forever grateful for you, Z!

Victoria: To know we have God as the foundation of our friendship is amazing to me. We literally met one another based on our relationship with God. I'm so glad we were able to grow a great friendship outside of the workplace and grow a connection based on the book *Relationship Goals* by Pastor Michael Todd. I hope we can continue to share a connection with one another, knowing God is at the center of it all.

Devinne/Destiny: My Twin Girls! I appreciate you both so much and for always being such great friends to me. You ladies are the true definition of beauty and brains! You all are so intelligent and smart and know what you all want out of life. Devinne, I'm thankful we have been able to be there for one another as it pertains to some of those hurtful relationships we endured together and helping each other out. Destiny, I thank you for always being so open to me and sharing those experiences in the hopes of growing from our pain and knowing what we deserve as women.

Ray: The true definition of a male best friend to me. You are always there to listen and give the best advice. During the span of our friendship, you always kept it real with me and always showed your loyalty to me.

You are such a great father and I pray you to receive whatever you want out of life.

Daisha: Since we have been friends, I have been able to learn so much from you. Not only have I learned so much from us being friends but I also learned how you always think outside the box. You give the best advice, and I often say, "This girl knows everything!" I'm so glad we were able to connect when we did to allow you to be a big part of my life while writing my book. God allowed us to be friends and connect at the most perfect time. Not only are you my neighbor, but will always be my friend.

Minister Kenyatta: Sis, you are such a wise individual. Watching you grow and become a minister has inspired me so much. You continue to allow God to use you as you preach His word. I pray things continue to work in your favor as you are obedient to God and allow Him to lead you.

Minister Jackie: Sis, I thank you for presenting me with a Bible at a time in my life when I needed God the most, in 2019. You gifting me with that bible has allowed me to grow into the woman of God I am today. I thank you for always being so positive and such a great help to women. I pray God continues to use you as you continue to spread His gospel.

Britny: Thank you Britny for always having such a great spirit. For always being so positive and such a great mother to your children. I pray you receive everything God has for you as you keep Him first. Just remember that God always gives us the desires of our hearts and just know our husbands are coming!

Chanice: I thank you so much for always being there for me when I was going through a tough time back in 2018-2019. You allow me to feel so comfortable around you and not feel ashamed to open up and tell my true feelings. I felt I could be so honest with you without any judgment. I look up to you as the woman of God you are to pave the way for me.

Amaris: Am, you have such a beautiful soul and have a beautiful voice to go along with it. I always say you have wisdom beyond your years because you have always been so mature to me. You are so driven and have no problem with going after what you want in life. I pray you to receive all of what you want out of life and continue to follow God because He will take you far.

Maddy: My protégé. I'm glad I have someone to look up to me, such as you. I want to set the best example for you to know that you can do whatever you put your mind to. I want you to know that if you can see it and dream it, then it's yours as long as you have faith in God. So, continue to be the smart young lady that you are, keep working hard, and you will receive whatever you dream of.

Olivia: I thank you for always being there whenever I need to talk. You are so smart and wise, and it shows through my niece Zoe. You are such an awesome Mom and always so willing to learn new ways how to enhance your mommy skills. I pray you continue to follow wherever God calls you to go, and I thank you for being there during the process of my book.

Shantana: My girl, who has gone from a coworker to a very good friend. I love how outspoken you are and never afraid to show your authentic self. You have always had my back and have been a great listening ear to me whenever I found myself in a dilemma. You are such a great educator and I pray God will continue to direct your path to do exactly what you want.

Alexandria: My Lexy Girl. I thank you for always understanding me and being my personal therapist. We are so similar in so many ways and you know exactly what to say to make me feel much better, always. When I was dealing with a lot, you were right there to give me the best advice and allow God to speak through you. I truly value our friendship that developed so fast.

Jasmin: Ever since I met you, you have been so sweet to me. When I first talked to you about my book, you were ecstatic. Your enthusiasm has shown me that I could make thousands of women feel the same way. Your happiness has truly pushed me to keep going and to know I can make a difference in other women's lives.

Bria Banks: No matter how long we go without talking, we always manage to pick back up where we left off. You have always set a great example for me. Because of you, I know that I can get whatever God has for me. If that's me standing in faith for my future husband, you allow me to know I can have it if it's in God's will.

Staci: No matter how far you move, we will always be great friends. Since we first met, we instantly became friends. You invited me to your wedding after knowing me for one week and I knew then we would be lifelong friends. I cherish our friendship and I'm glad I have you to look up to be the best mommy I can be to my future children.

Friends/Family: To the rest of my friends and family, I do this for you! I do this for us! I write this book to make a difference and let everyone know that we all can have that relationship with God and receive all that He has for us if we continue to trust and believe. I want to thank everyone who believed in me and continued to push me to keep going and know it's all possible.

Donnie & Molly: I thank you both for allowing me to get to where I am today. Without you two, I would not be an author and I would not have this wonderful relationship I have with my God today. You taught me that I don't need to depend on a man or a friend to be a whole woman but to solely depend on God.

HER: To you, to Her, I am HER! I want you to know I am just like you and you can truly do whatever you put your mind to. You can become a transformed woman with just a simple prayer. You can receive the very thing you dream of because dreams truly do come true. Allow God to build your faith and take you exactly where you need to go as you continue to follow Him. He wants to see you win and I want you to win too! Keep God first and He will truly give you the desires of your heart as long as you can trust and believe.

www.ingramcontent.com/pod-product-compliance
Lightning Source LLC
Chambersburg PA
CBHW021641120626
46545CB00002B/656